50 Savory Pie Recipes for Home

By: Kelly Johnson

Table of Contents

- Classic Chicken Pot Pie
- Beef and Mushroom Pie
- Spinach and Feta Quiche
- Shepherd's Pie
- Vegetable Pot Pie
- Salmon and Dill Pie
- Mushroom and Spinach Tart
- Beef Wellington
- Broccoli and Cheese Pie
- Ham and Cheese Quiche
- Turkey and Cranberry Pie
- Ratatouille Tart
- Bacon and Leek Pie
- Sweet Potato and Black Bean Pie
- Mediterranean Lamb Pie
- Rustic Vegetable Galette
- Chicken and Leek Pie
- Savory Pumpkin Pie
- Shrimp and Grits Pie
- Quinoa and Vegetable Pie
- Curried Lentil and Potato Pie
- Smoked Salmon Quiche
- Stuffed Bell Pepper Pie
- Spinach and Ricotta Pie
- Zucchini and Corn Pie
- Pork and Apple Pie
- Thai Chicken Curry Pie
- Caramelized Onion and Goat Cheese Tart
- Chorizo and Potato Pie
- Tomato and Basil Tart
- Beef and Ale Pie
- Asparagus and Gruyère Tart
- Chicken and Mushroom Pie
- Ratatouille Pot Pie
- Wild Mushroom and Thyme Pie
- Crab and Avocado Pie
- Cheesy Broccoli and Cauliflower Pie
- Moroccan Lamb Pie
- Pesto Chicken and Tomato Pie

- Italian Sausage and Peppers Pie
- Classic Quiche Lorraine
- Carrot and Potato Pie
- Spinach and Artichoke Pie
- Green Chile and Chicken Pie
- BBQ Pulled Pork Pie
- Artichoke and Parmesan Tart
- Egg and Bacon Pie
- Roasted Vegetable and Feta Pie
- Sweet Pea and Mint Tart
- Chicken Tikka Masala Pie

Classic Chicken Pot Pie

Ingredients:

- 1 pound cooked chicken, shredded
- 1 cup carrots, diced
- 1 cup peas
- 1/2 cup celery, diced
- 1/2 cup onion, diced
- 1/3 cup butter
- 1/3 cup all-purpose flour
- 1 3/4 cups chicken broth
- 2/3 cup milk
- Salt and pepper to taste
- 1 pie crust (store-bought or homemade)

Instructions:

1. Preheat oven to 425°F (220°C).
2. In a skillet, melt butter and sauté onion, celery, and carrots until soft.
3. Stir in flour, then gradually add chicken broth and milk. Cook until thickened.
4. Add shredded chicken and peas; season with salt and pepper.
5. Pour mixture into a pie crust, cover with a second crust, and seal edges. Cut slits in the top crust.
6. Bake for 30-35 minutes until golden brown.

Beef and Mushroom Pie

Ingredients:

- 1 pound ground beef
- 1 cup mushrooms, sliced
- 1 onion, diced
- 2 tablespoons Worcestershire sauce
- 1 teaspoon thyme
- Salt and pepper to taste
- 1 pie crust (store-bought or homemade)

Instructions:

1. Preheat oven to 400°F (200°C).
2. In a skillet, cook onion and mushrooms until soft. Add ground beef and cook until browned.
3. Stir in Worcestershire sauce, thyme, salt, and pepper.
4. Pour mixture into a pie crust, cover with another crust, and seal edges. Cut slits in the top.
5. Bake for 25-30 minutes until golden.

Spinach and Feta Quiche

Ingredients:

- 1 pie crust (store-bought or homemade)
- 1 cup spinach, chopped
- 1 cup feta cheese, crumbled
- 4 large eggs
- 1 cup heavy cream
- Salt and pepper to taste

Instructions:

1. Preheat oven to 375°F (190°C).
2. In a bowl, whisk together eggs, heavy cream, salt, and pepper.
3. Place spinach and feta in the pie crust, then pour egg mixture over the top.
4. Bake for 30-35 minutes until set and lightly golden.

Shepherd's Pie

Ingredients:

- 1 pound ground lamb (or beef)
- 1 cup carrots, diced
- 1 cup peas
- 1 onion, diced
- 2 tablespoons tomato paste
- 1 teaspoon Worcestershire sauce
- 4 cups mashed potatoes
- Salt and pepper to taste

Instructions:

1. Preheat oven to 400°F (200°C).
2. In a skillet, cook onion and carrots until soft. Add ground meat and cook until browned.
3. Stir in peas, tomato paste, Worcestershire sauce, salt, and pepper.
4. Transfer meat mixture to a baking dish and top with mashed potatoes.
5. Bake for 25-30 minutes until golden.

Vegetable Pot Pie

Ingredients:

- 2 cups mixed vegetables (carrots, peas, corn)
- 1/2 cup onion, diced
- 1/3 cup butter
- 1/3 cup all-purpose flour
- 1 3/4 cups vegetable broth
- 2/3 cup milk
- Salt and pepper to taste
- 1 pie crust (store-bought or homemade)

Instructions:

1. Preheat oven to 425°F (220°C).
2. In a skillet, melt butter and sauté onion until soft.
3. Stir in flour, then gradually add vegetable broth and milk. Cook until thickened.
4. Stir in mixed vegetables; season with salt and pepper.
5. Pour into pie crust, cover with another crust, seal edges, and cut slits on top.
6. Bake for 30-35 minutes until golden.

Salmon and Dill Pie

Ingredients:

- 1 pound salmon fillets, cooked and flaked
- 1/2 cup cream cheese, softened
- 1/4 cup fresh dill, chopped
- 4 large eggs
- 1 cup heavy cream
- Salt and pepper to taste
- 1 pie crust (store-bought or homemade)

Instructions:

1. Preheat oven to 375°F (190°C).
2. In a bowl, mix salmon, cream cheese, dill, eggs, heavy cream, salt, and pepper.
3. Pour mixture into pie crust and bake for 35-40 minutes until set and lightly golden.

Mushroom and Spinach Tart

Ingredients:

- 1 sheet puff pastry
- 1 cup mushrooms, sliced
- 1 cup spinach, chopped
- 1 onion, diced
- 4 large eggs
- 1 cup heavy cream
- Salt and pepper to taste

Instructions:

1. Preheat oven to 400°F (200°C).
2. Roll out puff pastry and place in a tart pan.
3. In a skillet, sauté onion and mushrooms until soft. Add spinach and cook until wilted.
4. In a bowl, whisk together eggs, heavy cream, salt, and pepper.
5. Add the vegetable mixture to the pastry, pour the egg mixture on top, and bake for 25-30 minutes until golden.

Beef Wellington

Ingredients:

- 1 pound beef tenderloin
- 8 oz mushrooms, finely chopped
- 1/4 cup pâté (optional)
- 1 sheet puff pastry
- 1 egg, beaten
- Salt and pepper to taste

Instructions:

1. Preheat oven to 400°F (200°C).
2. Sear the beef in a hot skillet until browned on all sides; season with salt and pepper.
3. In the same skillet, cook mushrooms until moisture evaporates. Let cool.
4. Roll out puff pastry and spread pâté over it (if using). Place beef in the center, top with mushrooms, and wrap the pastry around it.
5. Brush with beaten egg and bake for 25-30 minutes until golden brown. Let rest before slicing.

Enjoy these comforting and hearty dishes!

Broccoli and Cheese Pie

Ingredients:

- 2 cups broccoli florets, steamed
- 1 cup cheddar cheese, shredded
- 4 large eggs
- 1 cup heavy cream
- Salt and pepper to taste
- 1 pie crust (store-bought or homemade)

Instructions:

1. Preheat oven to 375°F (190°C).
2. In a bowl, mix steamed broccoli and cheese.
3. In another bowl, whisk eggs, heavy cream, salt, and pepper.
4. Combine broccoli mixture with egg mixture and pour into the pie crust.
5. Bake for 30-35 minutes until set and golden.

Ham and Cheese Quiche

Ingredients:

- 1 pie crust (store-bought or homemade)
- 1 cup diced ham
- 1 cup Swiss cheese, shredded
- 4 large eggs
- 1 cup milk
- Salt and pepper to taste

Instructions:

1. Preheat oven to 375°F (190°C).
2. In a bowl, whisk together eggs, milk, salt, and pepper.
3. Spread ham and cheese in the pie crust, then pour egg mixture on top.
4. Bake for 30-35 minutes until puffed and set.

Turkey and Cranberry Pie

Ingredients:

- 2 cups cooked turkey, shredded
- 1 cup cranberry sauce
- 1/2 cup onion, diced
- 1/2 cup celery, diced
- 1 teaspoon thyme
- 1 pie crust (store-bought or homemade)

Instructions:

1. Preheat oven to 375°F (190°C).
2. In a bowl, combine turkey, cranberry sauce, onion, celery, thyme, salt, and pepper.
3. Pour mixture into the pie crust, cover with a second crust, and seal edges.
4. Cut slits in the top and bake for 30-35 minutes until golden brown.

Ratatouille Tart

Ingredients:

- 1 sheet puff pastry
- 1 zucchini, sliced
- 1 eggplant, sliced
- 1 bell pepper, sliced
- 1 onion, sliced
- 2 cups marinara sauce
- 1 teaspoon Italian seasoning
- Olive oil for drizzling

Instructions:

1. Preheat oven to 400°F (200°C).
2. Roll out puff pastry and place it in a tart pan.
3. Spread marinara sauce on the pastry, then layer vegetables in a circular pattern.
4. Drizzle with olive oil, sprinkle with Italian seasoning, and bake for 30-35 minutes until vegetables are tender.

Bacon and Leek Pie

Ingredients:

- 1 pie crust (store-bought or homemade)
- 6 strips bacon, cooked and crumbled
- 2 leeks, sliced
- 4 large eggs
- 1 cup heavy cream
- Salt and pepper to taste

Instructions:

1. Preheat oven to 375°F (190°C).
2. In a skillet, sauté leeks until soft.
3. In a bowl, whisk together eggs, heavy cream, salt, and pepper.
4. Layer bacon and leeks in the pie crust, then pour egg mixture on top.
5. Bake for 30-35 minutes until set and lightly golden.

Sweet Potato and Black Bean Pie

Ingredients:

- 2 cups sweet potatoes, cooked and mashed
- 1 can (15 oz) black beans, rinsed and drained
- 1 teaspoon cumin
- 1 teaspoon chili powder
- 4 large eggs
- 1 pie crust (store-bought or homemade)

Instructions:

1. Preheat oven to 375°F (190°C).
2. In a bowl, combine mashed sweet potatoes, black beans, cumin, chili powder, and eggs. Mix well.
3. Pour mixture into the pie crust and bake for 30-35 minutes until set.

Mediterranean Lamb Pie

Ingredients:

- 1 pound ground lamb
- 1 onion, diced
- 1 cup spinach, chopped
- 1/2 cup feta cheese, crumbled
- 1 teaspoon oregano
- 1 pie crust (store-bought or homemade)

Instructions:

1. Preheat oven to 400°F (200°C).
2. In a skillet, cook lamb and onion until browned. Stir in spinach, feta, oregano, salt, and pepper.
3. Pour mixture into the pie crust, cover with another crust, seal edges, and cut slits in the top.
4. Bake for 30-35 minutes until golden.

Rustic Vegetable Galette

Ingredients:

- 1 pie crust (store-bought or homemade)
- 1 cup zucchini, sliced
- 1 cup bell pepper, sliced
- 1 cup cherry tomatoes, halved
- 1 teaspoon thyme
- Salt and pepper to taste
- Olive oil for drizzling

Instructions:

1. Preheat oven to 400°F (200°C).
2. On a floured surface, roll out the pie crust into a circle.
3. Arrange vegetables in the center, leaving a border. Sprinkle with thyme, salt, and pepper, and drizzle with olive oil.
4. Fold the edges over the filling, leaving the center exposed. Bake for 30-35 minutes until golden brown.

Enjoy these delicious pies and tarts!

Chicken and Leek Pie

Ingredients:

- 2 cups cooked chicken, shredded
- 2 leeks, sliced
- 1 cup chicken broth
- 1/2 cup heavy cream
- 1/3 cup butter
- 1/3 cup all-purpose flour
- Salt and pepper to taste
- 1 pie crust (store-bought or homemade)

Instructions:

1. Preheat oven to 375°F (190°C).
2. In a skillet, melt butter and sauté leeks until soft.
3. Stir in flour, then gradually add chicken broth and cream. Cook until thickened.
4. Add shredded chicken, salt, and pepper.
5. Pour into pie crust, cover with a second crust, seal edges, and cut slits on top.
6. Bake for 30-35 minutes until golden brown.

Savory Pumpkin Pie

Ingredients:

- 1 pie crust (store-bought or homemade)
- 2 cups pumpkin puree
- 1 cup heavy cream
- 3 large eggs
- 1 teaspoon garlic powder
- 1 teaspoon onion powder
- 1 teaspoon thyme
- Salt and pepper to taste

Instructions:

1. Preheat oven to 375°F (190°C).
2. In a bowl, whisk together pumpkin puree, cream, eggs, garlic powder, onion powder, thyme, salt, and pepper.
3. Pour the mixture into the pie crust.
4. Bake for 40-45 minutes until set.

Shrimp and Grits Pie

Ingredients:

- 1 cup grits, cooked
- 1 pound shrimp, peeled and deveined
- 1/2 cup cheddar cheese, shredded
- 1/4 cup green onions, chopped
- 1/2 cup cream
- 1 pie crust (store-bought or homemade)
- Salt and pepper to taste

Instructions:

1. Preheat oven to 375°F (190°C).
2. In a bowl, mix cooked grits, cheese, green onions, and cream.
3. Spread the mixture in the pie crust.
4. Sauté shrimp in a skillet until pink; season with salt and pepper.
5. Arrange shrimp on top of the grit mixture and bake for 25-30 minutes.

Quinoa and Vegetable Pie

Ingredients:

- 1 cup cooked quinoa
- 1 cup mixed vegetables (carrots, peas, corn)
- 4 large eggs
- 1/2 cup feta cheese, crumbled
- Salt and pepper to taste
- 1 pie crust (store-bought or homemade)

Instructions:

1. Preheat oven to 375°F (190°C).
2. In a bowl, mix quinoa, vegetables, eggs, feta, salt, and pepper.
3. Pour mixture into pie crust and bake for 30-35 minutes until set.

Curried Lentil and Potato Pie

Ingredients:

- 1 cup cooked lentils
- 1 cup mashed potatoes
- 1 onion, diced
- 2 cloves garlic, minced
- 2 tablespoons curry powder
- 1 pie crust (store-bought or homemade)

Instructions:

1. Preheat oven to 375°F (190°C).
2. In a skillet, sauté onion and garlic until soft. Add lentils, mashed potatoes, curry powder, salt, and pepper. Mix well.
3. Pour into pie crust and bake for 30-35 minutes until golden.

Smoked Salmon Quiche

Ingredients:

- 1 pie crust (store-bought or homemade)
- 4 large eggs
- 1 cup heavy cream
- 1 cup smoked salmon, chopped
- 1/2 cup dill, chopped
- Salt and pepper to taste

Instructions:

1. Preheat oven to 375°F (190°C).
2. In a bowl, whisk together eggs, cream, salt, and pepper.
3. Place smoked salmon and dill in the pie crust, then pour egg mixture on top.
4. Bake for 30-35 minutes until set and lightly golden.

Stuffed Bell Pepper Pie

Ingredients:

- 4 bell peppers, halved and seeded
- 1 pound ground beef or turkey
- 1 cup cooked rice
- 1 cup tomato sauce
- 1 cup shredded cheese
- Salt and pepper to taste
- 1 pie crust (store-bought or homemade)

Instructions:

1. Preheat oven to 375°F (190°C).
2. In a skillet, cook ground meat until browned; stir in rice, tomato sauce, salt, and pepper.
3. Stuff the bell pepper halves with the meat mixture and place in the pie crust.
4. Top with cheese and bake for 25-30 minutes until the peppers are tender.

Spinach and Ricotta Pie

Ingredients:

- 1 pie crust (store-bought or homemade)
- 2 cups spinach, cooked and chopped
- 1 cup ricotta cheese
- 1/2 cup mozzarella cheese, shredded
- 3 large eggs
- Salt and pepper to taste

Instructions:

1. Preheat oven to 375°F (190°C).
2. In a bowl, mix spinach, ricotta, mozzarella, eggs, salt, and pepper.
3. Pour mixture into pie crust and bake for 30-35 minutes until set and lightly golden.

Enjoy these delightful pies!

Chicken and Mushroom Pie

Ingredients:

- 2 cups cooked chicken, shredded
- 1 cup mushrooms, sliced
- 1 onion, diced
- 1/3 cup butter
- 1/3 cup all-purpose flour
- 1 cup chicken broth
- 1/2 cup heavy cream
- Salt and pepper to taste
- 1 pie crust (store-bought or homemade)

Instructions:

1. Preheat oven to 375°F (190°C).
2. In a skillet, melt butter and sauté onion and mushrooms until soft.
3. Stir in flour, then gradually add chicken broth and cream. Cook until thickened.
4. Add shredded chicken and season with salt and pepper.
5. Pour mixture into pie crust, cover with a second crust, seal edges, and cut slits on top.
6. Bake for 30-35 minutes until golden brown.

Ratatouille Pot Pie

Ingredients:

- 1 sheet puff pastry
- 1 zucchini, diced
- 1 eggplant, diced
- 1 bell pepper, diced
- 1 onion, diced
- 2 cups marinara sauce
- 1 teaspoon Italian seasoning
- Olive oil for drizzling

Instructions:

1. Preheat oven to 400°F (200°C).
2. In a skillet, sauté onion, zucchini, eggplant, and bell pepper until tender.
3. Stir in marinara sauce and Italian seasoning.
4. Pour mixture into a baking dish, cover with puff pastry, and cut slits for steam.
5. Bake for 25-30 minutes until the pastry is golden brown.

Wild Mushroom and Thyme Pie

Ingredients:

- 2 cups assorted wild mushrooms, sliced
- 1 onion, diced
- 2 tablespoons butter
- 1 teaspoon fresh thyme (or 1/2 teaspoon dried)
- 1/3 cup all-purpose flour
- 1 cup vegetable broth
- 1 cup heavy cream
- Salt and pepper to taste
- 1 pie crust (store-bought or homemade)

Instructions:

1. Preheat oven to 375°F (190°C).
2. In a skillet, melt butter and sauté onion and mushrooms until soft.
3. Stir in thyme, flour, and gradually add broth and cream; cook until thickened.
4. Pour into pie crust, cover with another crust, seal edges, and cut slits on top.
5. Bake for 30-35 minutes until golden.

Crab and Avocado Pie

Ingredients:

- 1 cup cooked crab meat
- 1 avocado, diced
- 1/2 cup cream cheese, softened
- 1 tablespoon lemon juice
- 2 green onions, chopped
- Salt and pepper to taste
- 1 pie crust (store-bought or homemade)

Instructions:

1. Preheat oven to 375°F (190°C).
2. In a bowl, mix crab meat, avocado, cream cheese, lemon juice, green onions, salt, and pepper.
3. Pour mixture into pie crust and bake for 20-25 minutes until heated through.

Cheesy Broccoli and Cauliflower Pie

Ingredients:

- 2 cups broccoli florets, steamed
- 2 cups cauliflower florets, steamed
- 1 cup cheddar cheese, shredded
- 4 large eggs
- 1 cup heavy cream
- Salt and pepper to taste
- 1 pie crust (store-bought or homemade)

Instructions:

1. Preheat oven to 375°F (190°C).
2. In a bowl, mix steamed broccoli, cauliflower, cheese, eggs, cream, salt, and pepper.
3. Pour mixture into pie crust and bake for 30-35 minutes until set and golden.

Moroccan Lamb Pie

Ingredients:

- 1 pound ground lamb
- 1 onion, diced
- 2 cloves garlic, minced
- 1 teaspoon cumin
- 1 teaspoon cinnamon
- 1/2 cup raisins
- 1/2 cup almonds, chopped
- 1 pie crust (store-bought or homemade)

Instructions:

1. Preheat oven to 400°F (200°C).
2. In a skillet, cook onion and garlic until soft, then add lamb and brown.
3. Stir in cumin, cinnamon, raisins, and almonds; season with salt and pepper.
4. Pour mixture into pie crust, cover with another crust, seal edges, and cut slits in the top.
5. Bake for 25-30 minutes until golden.

Pesto Chicken and Tomato Pie

Ingredients:

- 2 cups cooked chicken, shredded
- 1/2 cup pesto
- 1 cup cherry tomatoes, halved
- 1 cup mozzarella cheese, shredded
- Salt and pepper to taste
- 1 pie crust (store-bought or homemade)

Instructions:

1. Preheat oven to 375°F (190°C).
2. In a bowl, mix chicken, pesto, cherry tomatoes, and cheese. Season with salt and pepper.
3. Pour mixture into pie crust and bake for 25-30 minutes until bubbly and golden.

Italian Sausage and Peppers Pie

Ingredients:

- 1 pound Italian sausage, removed from casings
- 1 bell pepper, sliced
- 1 onion, sliced
- 1 teaspoon Italian seasoning
- 1 pie crust (store-bought or homemade)

Instructions:

1. Preheat oven to 400°F (200°C).
2. In a skillet, cook sausage, onion, and bell pepper until sausage is browned and vegetables are soft.
3. Stir in Italian seasoning and season with salt and pepper.
4. Pour mixture into pie crust, cover with another crust, seal edges, and cut slits in the top.
5. Bake for 25-30 minutes until golden.

Enjoy these delicious and hearty pies!

Classic Quiche Lorraine

Ingredients:

- 1 pie crust (store-bought or homemade)
- 6 slices bacon, cooked and crumbled
- 1 cup Swiss cheese, shredded
- 4 large eggs
- 1 cup heavy cream
- Salt and pepper to taste
- 1/4 teaspoon nutmeg (optional)

Instructions:

1. Preheat oven to 375°F (190°C).
2. In a bowl, whisk together eggs, cream, salt, pepper, and nutmeg.
3. Sprinkle bacon and cheese in the pie crust, then pour the egg mixture on top.
4. Bake for 30-35 minutes until set and golden brown.

Carrot and Potato Pie

Ingredients:

- 2 cups carrots, grated
- 2 cups potatoes, grated
- 1 onion, diced
- 4 large eggs
- 1 cup heavy cream
- Salt and pepper to taste
- 1 pie crust (store-bought or homemade)

Instructions:

1. Preheat oven to 375°F (190°C).
2. In a bowl, mix grated carrots, potatoes, onion, eggs, cream, salt, and pepper.
3. Pour mixture into the pie crust and bake for 35-40 minutes until golden.

Spinach and Artichoke Pie

Ingredients:

- 2 cups spinach, cooked and chopped
- 1 cup artichoke hearts, chopped
- 1 cup cream cheese, softened
- 1 cup mozzarella cheese, shredded
- 3 large eggs
- Salt and pepper to taste
- 1 pie crust (store-bought or homemade)

Instructions:

1. Preheat oven to 375°F (190°C).
2. In a bowl, combine spinach, artichokes, cream cheese, mozzarella, eggs, salt, and pepper.
3. Pour mixture into pie crust and bake for 30-35 minutes until set.

Green Chile and Chicken Pie

Ingredients:

- 2 cups cooked chicken, shredded
- 1 cup green chiles, diced
- 1 cup cheddar cheese, shredded
- 4 large eggs
- 1 cup heavy cream
- Salt and pepper to taste
- 1 pie crust (store-bought or homemade)

Instructions:

1. Preheat oven to 375°F (190°C).
2. In a bowl, mix chicken, green chiles, cheese, eggs, cream, salt, and pepper.
3. Pour mixture into pie crust and bake for 30-35 minutes until golden.

BBQ Pulled Pork Pie

Ingredients:

- 2 cups pulled pork
- 1 cup BBQ sauce
- 1/2 cup onion, diced
- 1 cup cheddar cheese, shredded
- 1 pie crust (store-bought or homemade)

Instructions:

1. Preheat oven to 375°F (190°C).
2. In a bowl, mix pulled pork, BBQ sauce, onion, and cheese.
3. Pour mixture into pie crust and bake for 25-30 minutes until heated through.

Artichoke and Parmesan Tart

Ingredients:

- 1 sheet puff pastry
- 1 cup artichoke hearts, chopped
- 1/2 cup Parmesan cheese, grated
- 2 large eggs
- 1 cup heavy cream
- Salt and pepper to taste

Instructions:

1. Preheat oven to 400°F (200°C).
2. Roll out puff pastry on a baking sheet and prick with a fork.
3. In a bowl, whisk together eggs, cream, salt, and pepper; add artichokes and Parmesan.
4. Pour mixture over pastry and bake for 25-30 minutes until golden.

Egg and Bacon Pie

Ingredients:

- 6 slices bacon, cooked and chopped
- 4 large eggs
- 1 cup milk
- 1 cup shredded cheese (cheddar or your choice)
- Salt and pepper to taste
- 1 pie crust (store-bought or homemade)

Instructions:

1. Preheat oven to 375°F (190°C).
2. In a bowl, whisk together eggs, milk, salt, and pepper.
3. Sprinkle bacon and cheese in the pie crust, then pour egg mixture on top.
4. Bake for 30-35 minutes until set and golden.

Roasted Vegetable and Feta Pie

Ingredients:

- 2 cups mixed vegetables (zucchini, bell peppers, carrots), roasted
- 1 cup feta cheese, crumbled
- 4 large eggs
- 1 cup heavy cream
- Salt and pepper to taste
- 1 pie crust (store-bought or homemade)

Instructions:

1. Preheat oven to 375°F (190°C).
2. In a bowl, mix roasted vegetables, feta, eggs, cream, salt, and pepper.
3. Pour mixture into pie crust and bake for 30-35 minutes until set.

Enjoy these delicious and comforting pies!

Sweet Pea and Mint Tart

Ingredients:

- 1 sheet puff pastry
- 2 cups fresh or frozen peas
- 1/2 cup fresh mint leaves, chopped
- 4 large eggs
- 1 cup heavy cream
- 1/2 cup feta cheese, crumbled
- Salt and pepper to taste

Instructions:

1. Preheat oven to 400°F (200°C).
2. Roll out puff pastry on a baking sheet and prick with a fork.
3. In a bowl, blend peas, mint, eggs, cream, feta, salt, and pepper until well combined.
4. Pour mixture into the pastry and bake for 25-30 minutes until golden and set.

Chicken Tikka Masala Pie

Ingredients:

- 2 cups cooked chicken, diced
- 1 cup tikka masala sauce (store-bought or homemade)
- 1/2 cup plain yogurt
- 1/2 cup frozen peas
- 1 teaspoon garam masala
- 1 pie crust (store-bought or homemade)

Instructions:

1. Preheat oven to 375°F (190°C).
2. In a bowl, mix diced chicken, tikka masala sauce, yogurt, peas, and garam masala.
3. Pour the mixture into the pie crust and bake for 25-30 minutes until heated through and the crust is golden.

Enjoy these flavorful tarts and pies!

www.ingramcontent.com/pod-product-compliance
Lightning Source LLC
LaVergne TN
LVHW081510060526
838201LV00056BA/3031